Thoughts at Midnight

From the Mind of Hurting Soul

Edward Bowers and Marsha Cain

This is a work of fiction. Names, characters, businesses, events, and incidents are the product of the author's imagination. Any resemblance to actual persons, living or dead, or actual events is purely coincidental.

Copyright © Edward Bowers, 2024

All rights reserved.

The moral rights of the author have been asserted.

No part of this book may be reproduced in any form on by any electronic or mechanical means, including information storage and retrieval systems, without permission in writing from the publisher, except by a reviewer who may quote brief passages in review.

Written by Edward Bowers

Inspired by Marsha Cains

First edition January 2024

I dedicate this book to
my sister-in-law. And my three exceptional children.
To the people, I have loved in the past.
Thank you all for the love and support you have shown me over the years.

Thoughts at Midnight
From the Mind of Hurting Soul

Table of Contents

Forward

      The thoughts or stories in this book are from the mind of a hurting 20-year-old soul a few years back. I had the honor of hearing these poems or stories from her older self. Reflecting on her meanings and interpretations. So relatable to my life. They may seem dark and depressing, or even just sad, but when you dig deep into even your tough times, you should be able to see the beauty in each one of these writings.

      We all have a dark side to ourselves, yet we hide it from sight. It takes strength to let that. darkness out. I have been told I have a lot of dark in me. That does not mean that I am evil or a bad person. I have just had things, like most of you, happen to me, mold me, and push me into this type of "dark" place in my head. Emotions are a tricky thing. This book is not here to help navigate those times but to enjoy.

These writings talk about love, and life struggles that
I hope will inspire you not to give up hope.

Edgar Allan Poe once said or wrote, "Tell me all the
terrible things you ever did, and let me love
you anyway." The meaning of the quote, Tell me every
terrible thing you ever did and let me love you
anyway; is the power of law and how it can transcend even
the darkest secrets. The Edgar Allan Poe
poem encourages us to be open and honest about our
mistakes and not to feel ashamed in the presence
of love.

While these things are from the mind of a 20-year-
old woman who battles with depression, and a few other
medical issues, please do not ignore the message in each
poem or story. Come
to read this book with an open mind and heart. There is no
judgment as she pours out her emotions
and feelings. I am so proud of her for putting these emotions
out for her personal growth and healing. I
am grateful she allowed me to pen this book with her help,
using her words on my pages.

I hope you enjoy what has been written here and
take the time to see the beauty and
relatability in every sentence. I hope this gives you a different
perspective on things that might happen
in your life.

Find the light in the darkness, or be it!

Thank you,
Edward Bowers

Love

Love to hate.
Hate to love.

Love with a Friend

Fell in love with a friend.
So bright and beautiful their face could be.
Funny and gentle their personality could see.
They fell out of love with this friend.
Now there is pain.
A dream that cannot be.
Maybe, just maybe
One day again they will want me.

Belong

Where do I belong?
Can I fly so high,
To Find where I belong?
Can I live so long to find
Where I belong?
As the days, months, years
Pass I have still not found
Where I belong.
Will it come to me
Or
Can I find that place?
So peace I can have
Where I belong.

A Love Lost

Love is lost.
What I thought I would find was a sign.
A sign, that there must be a plan.
A plan of evil,
Evil that will stay because
There can be no love with
A person who is lost.
They must find their way
Before love can arise,
But if they cannot prevail.
The love will be lost
Forever for all time.

As the Clock Ticks

As the clock ticks
In a room of silence.
In the distance I can hear the children playing.
They are playing a song.
A song of happiness.
It is so beautiful.
But than it fades.
Fades away slowly.
As the clocks ticking grows louder.
The lights grow dimmer.
And
The sound of bitter wind arises.
You can hear it beating against the walls.
As the clock ticks louder.
And.
Then it stops.
All is calm.
Again silence of the room.
As the clock ticks.

Reflection

As you look into the mirror what do you see?
I see the human nature that has
Baan created by Him.
He gives you this figure
To look at every day.
He lets you see the human
That He has made.
To understand yourself first
Is what He wants you to do.
And
Then to understand Him
And
Why He made you.

Death

Why is it in death
I find so much beauty?
It's so joyful.
Yet everyone else
Hates it or fears it.
I love it.
I see the life path to nothing.
Just to get old and die is pointless.
I see no future and hear no
Help.
So death is my only choice.
So peace can be my forward.

Locked in a Cage

Locked in a cage.
With walls of steal...
Boundaries to hard to knock over.
With only a pen
And
Paper.
To write, to wonder,
To talk too.
And
To dream in.
Locked in a cage.
You find no peace.
Just the silence and loneliness.
You find that the cage
Has no way out.
Now you know,
Your life will pass
You by,
Locked in this cage.

No Windows

No windows
Just mirrors.
You can hear them talk.
They are free.
Not trapped from freedom or
Life, love and sanity.
No windows
Just mirrors.
It shines so bright,
And blinds my life.
No hope to move,
No hope to be released.
No windows.
Just mirrors.
That have trapped me.

Seasons Changing

Cold days, the leaves
Start to change.
You can smell, taste, touch and hear
The seasons changing.
Your life changes with
Those seasons.
If you know it or not.
Watch, if you can,
Because one day your seasons
Will change.

Child of Beauty

How can a child of such beauty fade into
The ugly, dark bitter realm.
When he has never seen the light of life.
This light that glows so bright and beautiful
For them.
As the child wonders
Aimlessly through the world.
The child has some how found
The evils more comforting
But, why?
Rather then the light blue skies and the deep blue seas.
The child has strayed to the bareness of the brick world.
The child has no dreams of the green grass and clouds of
blue.
But only of hard cold metal bars and brick walls.
Yet, how did that beautiful child
Fade into dark, bitter, realm.
Yet to never have seen the light of life
That glows so bright and beautiful.

Soft Spoken Dreams

I close my eyes
And start to dream.
Wonder what can never be.
Those soft spoken dreams.
They come and go.
A life unknown;
Unknown to I,
Unknown to myself,
Unknown to me.
Are those soft, spoken dreams
Just known to my eyes?
Will they never come true?
How I wish to have.
Will they finally be true?

What Do They Know

What do they know;
How can they see?
See the person inside of me.
To tell me my feelings,
But to never fully experience.
To tell me to change a
Unchangeable thing.
What do they know?
How can they say;
Say I can have a peace and be ok
When they have never felt
Unbearable heartbreak.
Never felt the guilt, the terror and sadness.
All in one day.
The loneliness and coldness that comes over me.
This can only be felt by a person like me.
So what do they know?
How can they see,
See the loneliness taking over me.
The agene diapasons,
The harsh reality.
Only a person, a person like me can see.
So what can they say
I will be at peace and be ok
When they have never once experienced this unbearable pain.

Destiny

Do you believe in destiny?
The life you live is unchangeable.
Un reversable.
To wish to change this will never happen.
To wish to have this will never work.
Do you believe in destiny?
A line that cannot be crossed.
Walls that cannot be brought down.
This is destiny.
Destiny you cannot, will not, ever change.
Do you believe in destiny?

To Know

To know the only two things that listen.
Are things that cannot talk back.
I one day hope, to know
That it may talk back.
To answer what I cannot.

Missing

Are you going to miss
Me once I have moved on?
Are you going to miss me
Once I am gone?

No words

I have no words.
Only feelings.
Feelings I cannot
Explain.
Uncontrolled, untamed,
Unrecognized.
Why me with no words,
But only
Feelings?

Blank Pages

You start off with
No marks.
You start off with
No feelings.
Perfect and untouched.
No spots of ink.
Then it starts to fill the
Blank pages.
It starts to consume you.
Maybe it will be good, bad, or frightening.
It eats you alive.
It never stays perfect.
So many nights
I have tried to pray for someone to
Fix my pages.
Noone comes, there
Is no answer.
Will they ever come?
And
Answer my prayers?
Only more
Blank pages
To fill.

Beauty

Beauty.
Where does it lie?
Can you see beauty
Or
Do you have to look?
Is it just a pretty face
Or
What is underneath?
Will you ever really see
What beauty is?

Missing Out

I am missing
What I cannot have
And cannot catch.
Try as I might
It still doesn't happen.
Whishes of love.
So beautiful and bright.
Wishing of hope.
So I could have this in site.
I am still missing
What I cannot have.
Always and forever,
Of a life unplanned.

Lies

Lies of life,
Beauty, friends, family
And
Trust.
Lies so perfect.
They couldn't have been touched,
But now they have fallen.
Now no more lies,
Only truth.

I Wish

I wish there was a place.
A place where the seasons never change.
A place where time would stand still.
And love could prevail.
A place of hope
And dreams.
Dreams that come true.
I wish there was a place.
A place for me,
And you.

Different

To be different.
Does anyone know the feelings
To have to live?
A life of sorrow and madness.
They say you
Have to change.
But if you do.
You would still be different.
Still different,
And
Alone.

Wrong

I have been wrong.
Wronged by me.
And wronged by others.
I have shamed myself
And
Embarrassed myself.
My knowledge,
My ugliness
And
My life.
I have put on my face.
Painted it well.
Never to show the trueness of me.
I have been wrong.
Wronged by others.
I have thought of others
As friends for life,
As lovers,
And
As comforts.
I have been wrong.
Wronged by others.

My Identity

My identity I do not know.
To find it I must travel.
I must go.
When the journey ends and still I have found
No hope.
Then I must travel again.
Life will keep going and so will I.
So, finding myself takes forever.
Then forever I must go.

Justice

Did you give
Justice?
Justice to me.
Did you give
Justice?
Justice to he?
Did you give
Justice?
Justice to she?
Did you give
Justice?
That hurt them
And
Me.

To Find Yourself

I find myself looking for myself.
Rather than just being myself.
Confusing yes but, understandable.
The questions always ringing in my head.
Who am I?
Why am I here?
What should I be or act like?
Is this real?
Yet the question remains.
And
Still, I wonder
Why I am looking at myself rather than just being myself?
Confusing yes, but understandable.
Yet I still walk alone looking for me.
Or maybe someone accepting of me.
But, yet I grow lost and tired.
The journey so long
And
The question still remains.
Why am I looking for myself rather?
Then just being myself?
Confusing yes but, understandable.

Earth Yells

The wind blows harder
As the day grows older.
And
I sit in my room.
And
Look out the window into the
Dark, damp winter.
As the wind beats up against the window;
I wonder why the earth yells so loudly.
Why is she so upset, cold and bitter?
Yet, I know when the snow falls, and all is calm she
Will be happy again.
Only on a lovely winters eve.

The Edge

I am about to fall.
Fall off the edge.
Into a deep sleep.
Where I can find
Peace.
I am about to fall.
Fall off the edge
Doesn't seem so bad.
Maybe it would
Be better
Then this realm.
I am about to fall.
Fall off the edge
And
Can not be stopped
If I choose
To go to the
Edge.

Silent

So silent is the incant boy.
He does not speak.
Just works and then he leaves.
Bringing his baseball.
And walking home alone.
So silent is the incant boy.
He knows not of drugs and alcohol.
He does not hear, speak or sue any evil.
So silent is the incant boy.
I wonder if he will see any of this evil.

Pure

So pure is she.
Lovely as can be.
Not just on the outside.
But there inside as well.
Kind and gentle.
So willing to help.
So pure inside.
You can see right
Through her
Speaking of happiness
And pure love that can be.
What love she brings
To you and me.

Fallen

I have fallen
From flying so high.
I have fallen
From the sky.
Why can't I go on
And fly so high?
I will keep moving.
It's what I must do.
Because I will fly again.
In that sky of blue.
If it takes forever,
Forever to do.

Questions That Cannot be Answered

Love
What I would give to?
Have that feeling again.

Doors
Behind every door there
Is no light?
Only darkness...

Missing
Why do I miss something
I cannot have?

Life
Why do I miss something
I cannot have?

Money
All the money in the world can't buy my happiness,
But someone who cares can. Why?

Pictures

Looking at the pictures.
Wonder why are they there?
Seeing that they don't fit.
Nor do they care.
None of them heard from.
As I look at my pictures.
And
Know
I am unheard
Of.

A Dream

Pure happiness.
Blue sky's, white clouds.
A life of forgiveness.
A dream to be found.
Trees of colors
And seasons so bright.
Children of happiness
And never any fight.
A dream of love
With blue sky's and white clouds.
A dream of happiness
That will be found.

Lose Your Dreams

When you are missing
A piece of your life
You may wonder.
Why?
You try to find it
But you always fail.
Then you go to sleep and
Never dream not one single dream.
Then you awake and try to find
What you have been missing.
All it really is;
Is one little dream.
If you lose this
You will lose your sanity.
Always to be looking
But, never to find.
This will occur
Forever and all times.
So take this in mind and
Remember your dreams because
They are your life.
Your support and sanity.

Friends

What are friends?
Is there any you know?
What does it mean?
How do you know?
Who do you trust?
Where do they go?
And why do they leave
If they are a friend?
What are friends?
Why do they hurt you?
Why are they deceitful?
Are these not friends?
But only my enemies.
Did I keep them close not
To be hurt?
And in the end
Got burned.
What are friends?
Maybe there is none.
Maybe they are the wrong ones?
Will you and I ever really know?
What are friends?

Bitch

You're a bitch.
Want to know why?
You can't keep a secret
And always lie.
You extend the truth
And
Sell it away.
To hurt friends
And
All your prey.
You find joy in
Life from
Being this way.
This makes you
A bitch!
Now you better look out.
Because this I will tell you.
What goes around comes around.
And it's headed straight for you.

Truth

True never hurts you.
Always listens
Never fails you.
True
Truly loves you.
No matter what.
You say or do.
True helps you through
Hard times.
True is faithful
And
True is happiness.
True will always be there.
Because true really does love you.

Screaming

Screaming so loud
The walls start to shake.
Screaming so loud.
Window start to break.
Can't anyone hear or help
Can anyone stop the pain and hurt that is felt?
Screaming so loud.
No one seems to hear.
Can't any one help so I can find peace in here.
Peace
In here.

What I Would Give For Love

What I would give for love to find me.
That feeling of
Happiness, hope, sanity.
I give up my life if it would happen to me.
I would give up my soul
If I could only be.
What I would give for love to find me.
So once in this world
I would have something.
And be able to see the life inside me.

Reflections

As you look into the mirror what do you see.
I see the human nature that has
Been created by Him.
He gives you this figure
To look at every day.
He lets you see the human
That He has made.
To understand yourself first
Is what He wants you to do
And
Then to understand Him
And
Why He made you.

What I would Give for Love

What I would give to find me.
That feeling of
Happiness, hope, and sanity.
I'd give up my life if it would happen.
I would give up my soul,
If only it could be.
What I would give for love to find me.
So once in this world.
I could have peace of mind.
And be able to see the life in me.
Love does not prevail its' only dream.
What I would give for love to find me.
It does not matter can't you see
Because of the life that was given
To me.

Why Me?

Why me? Why me?
To suffer a life of unchangeable pain.
To walk this world sad and untamed
With no answers to the questions.
And no rhymes or reasons.
Why
Try to look up, but only to fall.
Try to break through, but always fall.
Why me?

A Dark Winters Day

A candle, a light
To save that dark day.
Not found, never captured.
Never seen in anyway.
Not one cent of beauty to brighten these eyes.
Only dark cold, madness from these gray skies.
Just having to wait is what you must do.
Wait and want.
Until the sun will shine through.

Looking Out the Window

Staring out the window.
My mind starts to wonder.
It goes to a place,
A place for me to pounder.
It's only that I realize it's not just a place to wonder
Escape.
Where dreams, of colds of blue,
Rainbows of colors, and a sun shining through.

A Lonely Life

A dark, cold place...
Where only the voices
Of the dead can be heard.
I whisper into the air to try to find my way.
From the path that I have strayed.
Nothing...
Only silence to find the way to the bright beautiful path.
So hard, so lonely.
No one to help.
And all you hear is the voices
Of the dead in the this dark cold place.

Hurting

Why would they hurt?
If they loved
Long time friendship.
Come once in a lifetime.
Then you hurt.
You hurt people.
And
They suffer.
Why would they hurt you?
Why would you hurt them?
How could they hurt you?
How could you hurt them?
To be so harassed
And
Then to gossip
And
Be happy.
How could they?
How could you?
Longtime friends
Never speak again.
How could it change
So fast?
Is this what life is?
Or
A choice?

Thank You

I could not find you.
Something was wrong.
I searched and searched.
I tried to see but blind for so long.
But I always failed.
Then it hit me.
You didn't even care.
I cried for nights in complete despair.
Then I realized.
If this is a friend
What are my enemies
Like.
I thank you for this.
For leaving my site
So I could find truth
That there's
No one but me
And
That's all I ever really need.
So again
Thank you,
For leaving me.

Work

Workers work
Buzzing like bees,
Wonder when they
Day will end.
Try not to fight
The madness of the day.
Working so hard to pass the time away.
As the workers
Work buzzing like bees.

The Seasons of a Friend

There was this girl I used to know.
She was unique in every way.
She has a cool house and
Went through a lot of pain.
She wears the "in" clothes,
The cool hair.
She had a lot of friends.
Lives in a house
Not far away and watches a baby
Every day.
You can talk to her
And she will answer.
She would help you when you were
Down and could not find a way.
But watch she has faded.
Faded away.
Not because of you
Not because of me.
Just because her
Seasons have changed.

Caring

To care is to feel.
Feel life, happiness
And
Joy.
You love living
If you care for someone
Or
Something.
Euphoria comes to you.
When they stop caring
For your pain, unbearable
Pain runs through you.
Life changes.
You stop caring.
But would this be better
Then you will never hurt.
You will just be numb.
And
Life changes again.

Forgiveness

Forgive me I have sinned.
Sinned against you Lord.
Lied to myself, family
And more.
Forgive this life or terror
And
Pain.
Please so I can be free again.
Father when you pray
Please pray for me.
Pray for my soul.
So that I can be free.

Thank You

I could not find you.
Something was wrong.
I searched and searched
But I always fell.
Then it hit me.
You did even care.
I cried for days,
And nights.
Then I realized
If this is a friend
What are enemies
Like.
Thank you for this.
For leaving my site.
So I could find truth.
No one but me.
And
That's all I will ever need.
So again.
Thank you,
Thank you for leaving me.

Hiding

Why do they hide?
Where do they go?
Why do they lock
Themselves in.
Nobody knows.
To know you're not wanted
And
Know you'll never really be.
It makes you wonder
Why don't you just'
Shoot me.

Face

Show your face.
Don't push me away.
Let me see the trueness
You have for me.
don't hide away
in the dark, cold place.
You can
Show your face.
Let me see.
So I can come to know
And
See the heart you have for me.
A heart so big,
That fills the sky.
Please don't hide.

Love and Beauty

Soft and beautiful.
In every little way.
Will cuddle with you.
Loves to play.
Whishes to be around you
And
Never leaves your side.
He sees what we
Cannot.
Cannot say a word.

Epolouge

A little change from my normal writings I understand. Yet still from the heart. Still authentic, I hope. We are not having a pity party, nor is this a cry for attention. This is just the thoughts that came to a young woman at midnight. Thoughts of a hurting soul. Love and pain of a person that felt alone and unloved, yes like me. But it is better to write it out than to hold it in and allow it to bottle up and consume yourself.

I hope for her that she finds peace and love in her life, a love that it more of that "pragma" type of love. I wish and hope and pray the same for you all, as well as myself. The kind of love that that we all are worthy of and deserve.

"Pragma" love is that committee, long lasting love most people dream of. In the simplest of terms, it is love that looks long-term.

It is built on commitment, endurance, true companionship, and sharing similar hopes for the future, which includes things like building a family and putting down roots. That is correct, this is the "married folks" kind of love. The kind you will do anything for. If you are married, I am sure you get it. This is the love that you are willing to just 'make it work" no matter what. Yes, there will be ups and downs. But aren't we all looking for that partner that will not leave us, even in our dark time? Yes, it will be a lot of work, but it is worth it.

So again, I hope you see the beauty in these writings, and if you too feel this way don't allow anyone to say you are too dark and negative.

If you are hurting because this "pragma" love seems to be ever escaping from your grasp? Unfortunately, it may be, but keep searching for it. Don't give up, I have not, and I am 45 years old. **Make it work!** I mean seriously, who doesn't want that person in their life, that even at 60 or 70 or hell even 80-years -old that will hold their hand, and look at them the same way they did when they first met?

Possibly you have that already and are reading this little book. Congratulations, I am happy for you. So maybe these "poems" read differently for you. I don't know what each poem means to each reader of this book. Maybe it will help you treat someone in your life more compassionately, say your child.

Whatever these words spoke to you, take them to heart. Let them help you grow in your relationships.

Protect the ones you love.

I hope you enjoyed this book and found the beauty in it. I know I did when I heard her story.

www.ingramcontent.com/pod-product-compliance
Lightning Source LLC
Chambersburg PA
CBHW031327130726
47988CB00007B/3017